YOU CAN MASTER MATH!

Let's Add and Subtract

By Mike Askew

PowerKiDS press
New York

Published in 2022 by The Rosen Publishing Group, Inc.
29 East 21st Street, New York, NY 10010

Editors: Ruth Owen and Mark J. Sachner
Designer: Emma Randall

Images courtesy of Ruby Tuesday Books and Shutterstock.

Cataloging-in-Publication Data
Names: Askew, Mike.
Title: Let's add and subtract / Mike Askew.
Description: New York : PowerKids Press, 2022. | Series: You can master math!
Identifiers: ISBN 9781725331556 (pbk.) | ISBN 9781725331570 (library bound) | ISBN 9781725331563 (6 pack) | ISBN 9781725331587 (ebook)
Subjects: LCSH: Addition--Juvenile literature. | Subtraction--Juvenile literature.
Classification: LCC QA115.A85 2022 | DDC 513.2'11--dc23

Manufactured in the United States of America

CPSIA Compliance Information: Batch #CSPK22.
For Further Information contact Rosen Publishing, New York, New York at 1-800-237-9932.

Contents

Ladybug, Ladybug

The ladybug needs some spots.

Get Ready

You will need:
- Buttons or counters

Use some buttons or counters to put the same number of spots on each wing.

How many spots does your ladybug have altogether?

Now put a different number of spots on your ladybug. Make sure each wing has the same number of spots.

Make a Prediction

Take a handful of your counters.

How many do you have?

Can you use that number of counters to put spots on the ladybug so that each wing has the same number and there are no counters left over?

Put the counters on the ladybug's wings and check your prediction.

Four's Fantastic Facts

Numbers that can be split exactly into two equal groups are called **even numbers**. The other numbers are called **odd numbers**.

Zigzag Numbers

Get Ready

You will need:
- A sheet of paper
- Scissors
- A pen or pencil

1. Cut a strip of paper about 2 inches (5 cm) wide off the long side of the paper.

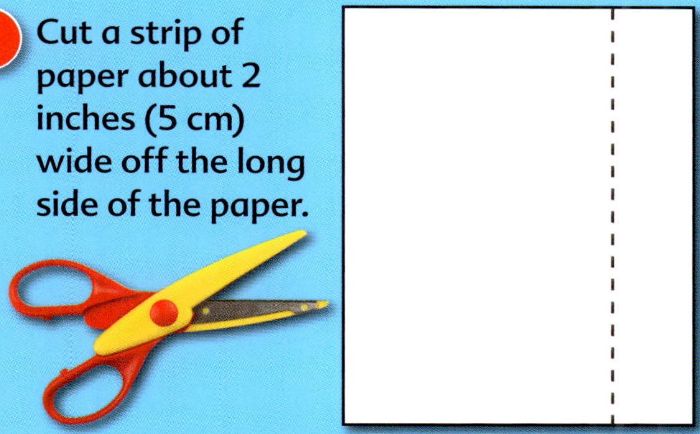

2. Fold the strip in half. Fold it again. And again.

3. Open it up and reverse some of the folds to make a zigzag strip.

4. Write the numbers 1 to 8 on your strip.

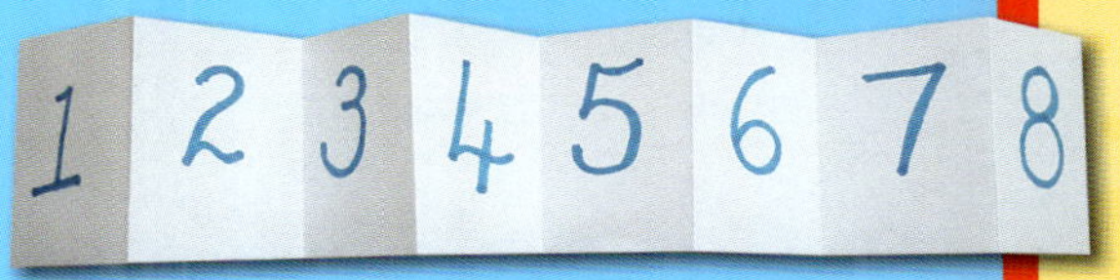

5. Now, stand your strip on the table so that you can only see the **even numbers**.

6. Now move the strip so that you can only see the **odd numbers**.

Go For It!

Try cutting and folding a longer strip.

What are the even numbers up to 20?

What are the odd numbers?

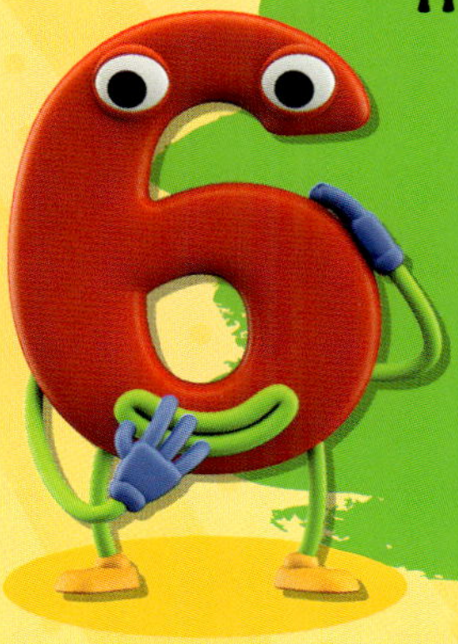

Shape Numbers

Get Ready

You will need:
- Buttons or counters

Take 16 counters and arrange them to make a square.

Sixteen is a **square number.**

What other numbers can be square? Use your counters to investigate.

Arrange 15 counters to make a triangle.

Fifteen is a **triangular number.**

What other numbers can be triangular? Use your counters to investigate.

GO For It!

Can you find a number that is square AND triangular?

Let's Play Pick Up

Get Ready

You will need:

- 10 small objects, such as buttons, counters, or paper clips
- A friend to play with

1. Put the 10 objects on the table in a row.

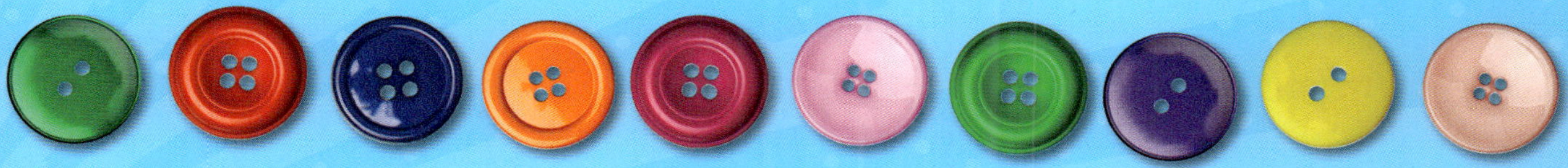

2. Player One picks up and removes either 1 or 2 objects.
3. Player Two can now pick up and remove 1 or 2 objects.
4. Take it in turns to pick up and remove 1 or 2 objects.
5. The winner is the player who picks up the LAST object!

Four's Fantastic Facts

If you go first, you can ALWAYS win this game. Can you figure out how?

Go For It!

Try playing with 15 objects. Now you can pick up 1, 2, or 3 each time.

Pick Up 6

Get Ready

You will need:
- 2 dice
- 12 counters
- A sheet of paper
- A pencil or pen
- A friend to play with

1. Draw a playing board of 12 squares, numbered 1 to 12.
2. Each player takes six counters. Then each player puts their counters alongside a number on their side of the board. For example:

3. Player One rolls the two dice and adds the scores. If they have a counter on that number, they take it off the board.

4. Next, Player Two rolls both dice, adds the scores and removes a counter if they can.
5. Keep taking it in turn, and the winner is the first player to take off all their counters!

Go For It!

You can put more than one counter on a number. Are there good numbers to put more than one counter on?

Are there any numbers you do not want to put a counter on?

Combine 4

Get Ready

You will need:

- 4 dice (if you only have one die, you can roll it four times and write down the number each time)
- Paper and a pen or pencil (for recording your calculations)

Begin by rolling your four dice.

What different numbers can you make using exactly three of your dice scores? You can add or subtract the scores. For example:

2 + 3 + 5 = 10

2 + 3 + 6 = 11

Look at the totals. That's 10, 11 in order.

Can you use your dice scores to make a string of numbers in order? For example:

2 + 5 − 6 = 1

3 + 5 − 6 = 2

6 + 2 − 5 = 3

That's 1, 2, 3 in order.

What is the longest string of numbers you can make with your dice scores?

Go For It!

The scores on these dice are all 4.

How many different numbers can you make by adding or subtracting all four 4s?

Dartboard Challenge

To take the dartboard challenges, you will use counters to be your darts.

Get Ready

You will need:

- 3 counters
- Paper and a pen or pencil

Challenge 1

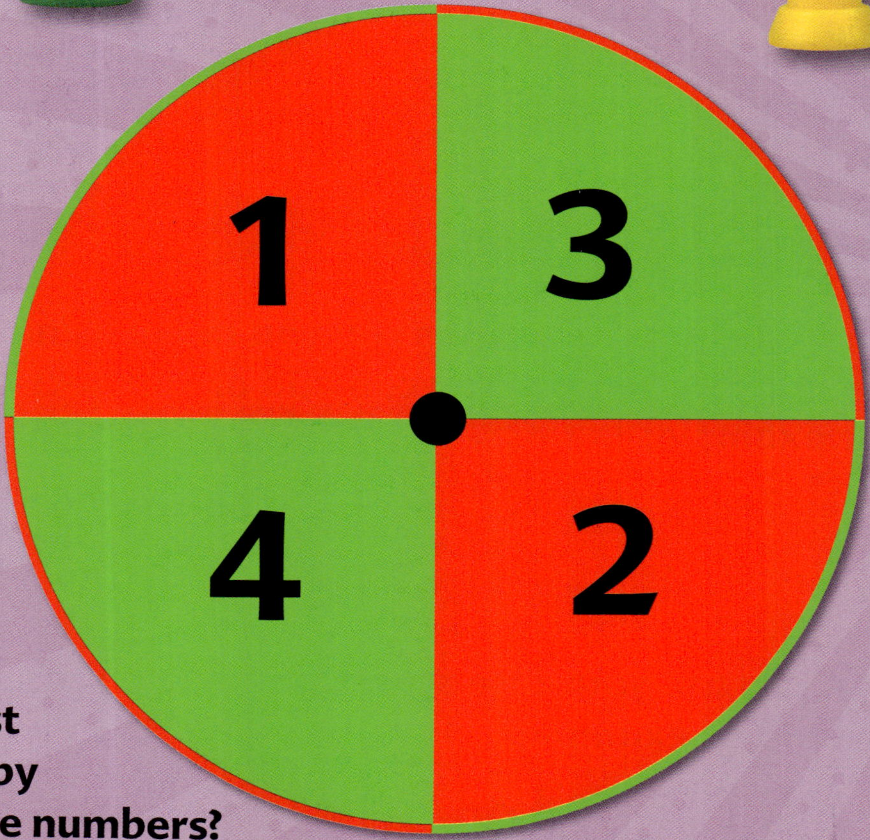

Take your three darts and place them on the dartboard.

All three darts have to be on the board.

You can have more than one dart on a number.

What is the highest score you can get by adding up the three numbers?

Challenge 2

Look at the numbers on this dartboard. Can you score exactly 10 using three darts?

Place each dart in a section on the dartboard.

All three darts have to be on the board.

You can have more than one dart on a number.

GO FOR IT!

3 is the lowest score you can get on this dartboard. 18 is the highest score.

How many of the numbers between 3 and 18 can you score with 3 darts?

Domino Challenge

To play these games you will need a set of dominoes.

10 Square

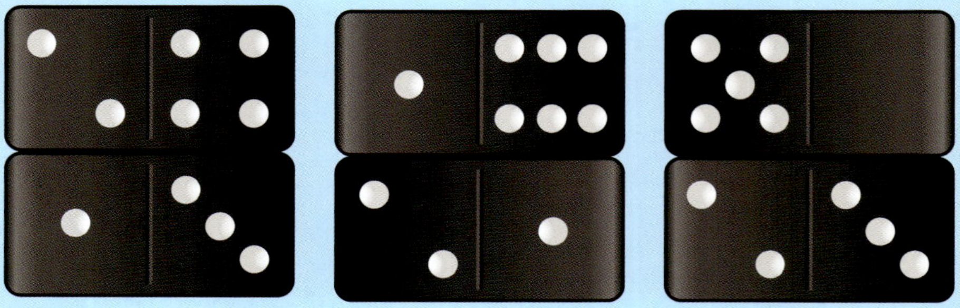

What do you notice about these domino squares?

The total number of spots in each square is 10.

Make some more domino 10 squares.

How many can you find?

Make 12

The dots on these two sets of dominoes add up to 12.

Can you make a set of dominoes where the dots add up to 12?

What is the biggest set of dominoes you can make with a total of 12 dots? What is the smallest set?

How many sets like this can you make?

What's My Rule?

You will need a friend to play this game.

1. Place all the dominoes face up on the table.

2. Make up a secret number rule for sorting the dominoes.

3. Your friend chooses a domino.

   If the domino fits your rule, your friend puts it face up in front of them.

   If the domino does not fit your rule, they put it face up in front of you.

4. Your friend keeps choosing dominoes and must try to work out what your rule is.

5. Once they've guessed the rule, count the number of dominoes they have collected. That number is their score.

6. Place all the dominoes back on the table. Now it's your friend's turn to think of a rule and you must work out what it is. Can you do this in fewer guesses than your friend and collect fewer dominoes?

   The winner is the player with the lowest score.

Ideas for Rules

Here are some rules you can use, or you can make up your own.

A domino must have a 3 on it.

The total number of dots on a domino must be an even number.

The total number of dots on a domino is greater than 6.

There is a difference of 2 between the dots on each side of a domino.

Let's Make 10

Your challenge in this game is to make pairs of cards that add up to 10.

Get Ready

You will need:

- A pack of playing cards with the picture cards taken out (Aces count as the number 1)

1. Shuffle, or mix up, the cards.
2. Lay out the top eight cards from the pack faceup in a two-by-four grid.

Can you find a pair of cards that add up to 10?

3. If you can find a pair of cards that add up to 10, cover them with two new faceup cards. If there are two 10s showing, cover this pair with two new faceup cards.
4. Keep covering pairs of cards.

Can you deal out all of the cards?

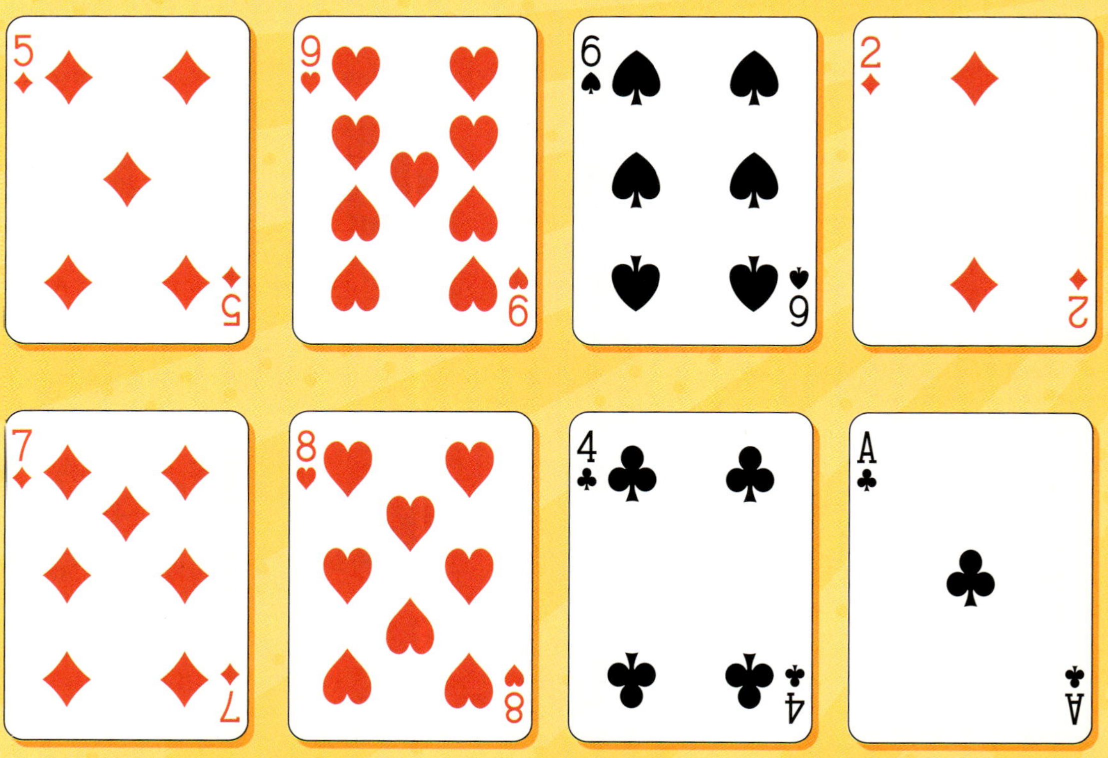

Let's Play Fish

In this game, you must collect pairs of numbers that add up to 10 — against an opponent!

Get Ready

You will need:

- 18 cards (1 to 9 from two different suits)
- A friend to play with

1. Shuffle, or mix up, the cards.
2. Place all the cards facedown on the table in a three-by-six grid.

3. You go first. Turn two cards face up. If the two cards add up to 10, pick up both cards and keep them.
4. If the cards do not add up to 10, turn them back over.
5. Now it is your friend's turn. Your friend turns over two cards and if the cards add up to 10, they keep them.
6. The game is over when all the cards have been picked up. The winner is the player with the most cards!

Magic Dice

Look at a die. The numbers on the opposite sides always add up to 7.

1 + 6 = 7

2 + 5 = 7

3 + 4 = 7

This fact can be used to amaze your friends!

Get Ready

You will need:

- 3 dice
- A pen and paper

1. Give your friend the three dice and a pen and paper. Turn around so you cannot see the dice.
2. Tell your friend to stack the dice on top of each other. Explain that five numbers now can't be seen.
3. Ask your friend to peek at the five hidden numbers and write them down. Next, your friend should add up the hidden numbers and write down the total. Finally, they should fold up the paper so you can't see the total.
4. Turn around. Ask your friend to hold the paper to their forehead and think of the total.
5. Look at the number facing upward on the very top of the dice tower. Subtract that number from 21. The answer will be the total written on the paper. Say the number and amaze your friend!

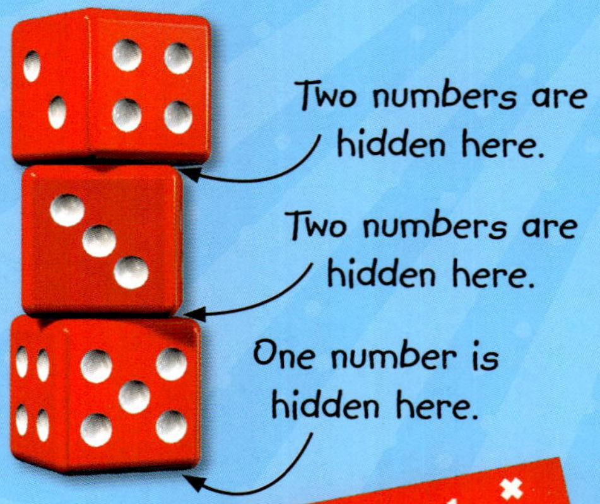

Go For It!

Can you figure out how the numbers on a die make the magic trick work?

Number Poem

What's your favorite number?

Write a poem about a number.

Your poem should have five lines.

The first four lines all start with your favorite number.

Get Ready

You will need:

- Paper and a pen or pencil

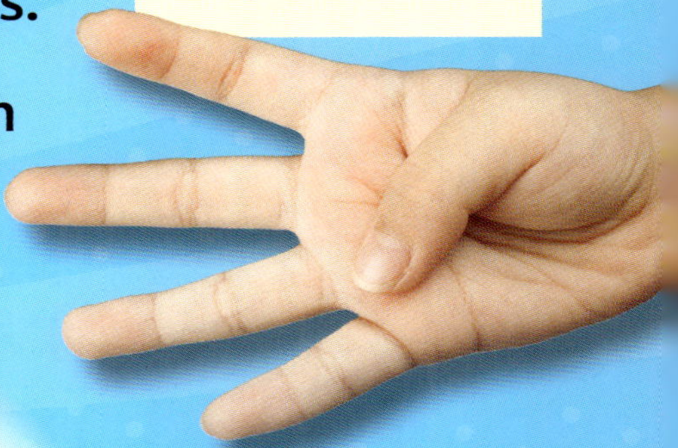

Two

Two eyes that peer
Two ears that hear
Two hands that hold
Two feet too cold
So many twos

What's Your Name's Number?

Get Ready

You will need:

- Some paper with squares
- A pen or pencil

Write down the alphabet.

Then give each letter a number from 1 to 26.

a	b	c	d	e	f	g	h	i	j	k	l	
1	2	3	4	5	6	7	8	9	10	11	12	
n	o	p	q	r	s	t	u	v	w	x	y	z

Write down your name.

Under each letter write the matching number.

G	r	a	c	e
7	18	1	3	5

Add up the numbers to find your name's number.

$$7 + 18 + 1 + 3 + 5 = 34$$

Go For It!

Whose name has the biggest number in your family?

Can you find a name or word that adds up to exactly 100?

Five Steps to 50

Your challenge is to get as close to 50 as possible in five steps of 10 or 1.

Get Ready

You will need:
- A die
- Paper and a pen or pencil

1. Roll the dice twice and write down the scores.

2. Use the scores to make two 2-digit numbers. For example, if you roll a 3 and a 5 you can make:

35 **53**

These are your starting numbers.

3. Take one of your starting numbers. You can add or subtract 10 or 1 to this starting number.

4. Do this exactly five times.

How close to 50 can you get?

5. Now do this with the other starting number. Which starting number gets you closer to 50?

35

Step 1: 35 + 10 = 45
Step 2: 45 + 10 = 55
Step 3: 55 – 1 = 54
Step 4: 54 – 1 = 53
Step 5: 53 – 1 = 52

53

Step 1: 53 + 10 = 63
Step 2: 63 – 10 = 53
Step 3: 53 – 1 = 52
Step 4: 52 – 1 = 51
Step 5: 51 – 1 = 50

Spot on!

Five a Side

Using the counters, can you make each side of the triangle add up to 5?

Get Ready

You will need:

- Counters
- Paper and a pen or pencil

Start putting counters in the circles. If you wish, a circle can have zero counters.

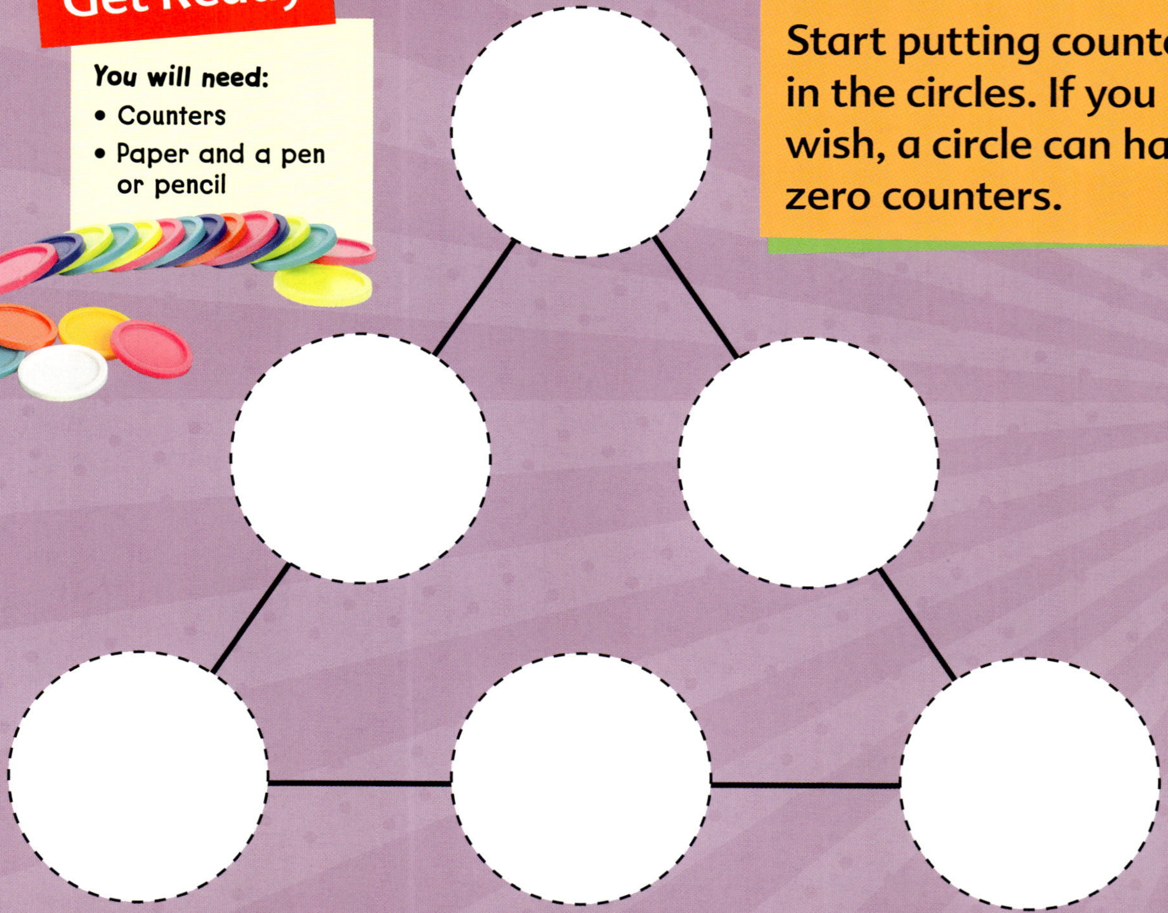

Remember, the number of counters on each side of the triangle must add up to 5.

How many counters did you use altogether?

Can you find a solution using fewer counters? Or more counters?

GO FOR IT!

How many different solutions can you find?

Can you make each side of the triangle add up to 10?

Make 15

Get Ready

You will need:

- Playing cards 1 to 9 (Aces count as 1)
- A big sheet of paper
- A pencil or pen

1. On the sheet of paper draw a three-by-three grid. It should be big enough to put a playing card in each section.
2. Shuffle, or mix up, your cards.
3. Turn the top card over. Put it in one of the squares of your grid.
4. Your challenge is to put the 9 cards on your grid and make 15 in as many ways as possible by adding three cards in a row. The rows can be across, down or diagonal.
5. Turn over the next card and put it on your grid.
6. Keep turning over cards and adding them to the grid.

When all 9 cards are on the grid, how many 15s can you find?

At the Corners

Get Ready

You will need:

- Paper and a pen or pencil

Draw a triangle on your sheet of paper.

Write a number in your triangle. For example, 15.

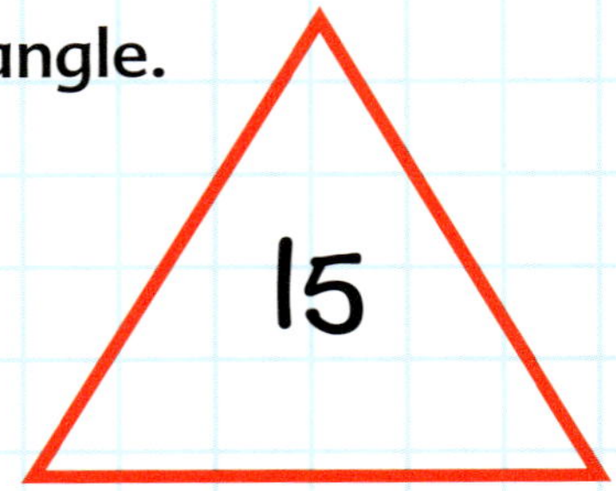

How many different ways can you find to put different numbers at the corners that always add up to 15?

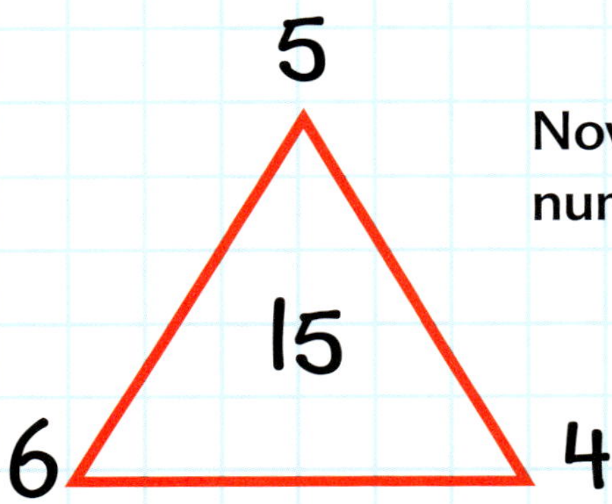

Now try again with a different number inside the triangle.

Go For It!

Draw a square instead of a triangle.

Write a number in the middle.

Find four numbers to go on the square's corners that add up to the number in the middle.

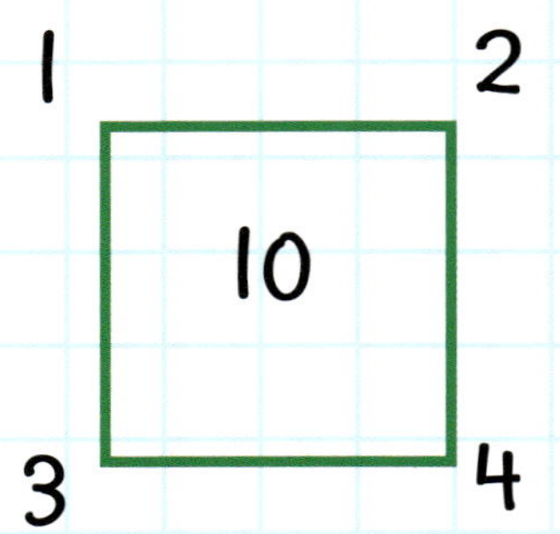

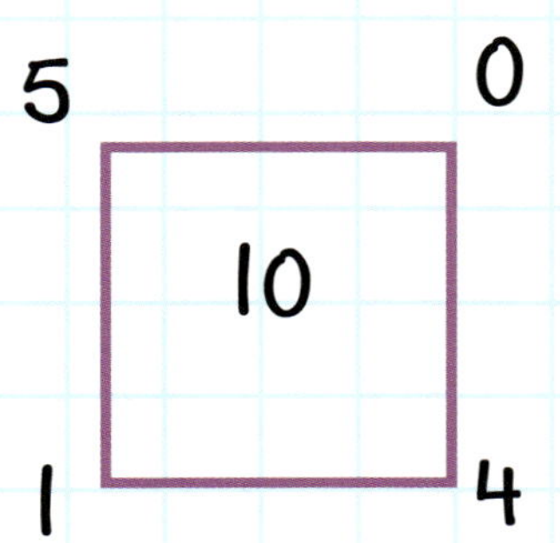

What's the Difference?

Get Ready

You will need:

- Paper and a pen or pencil

Get ready to play by drawing a large square.

1. Write a different number at each corner of the square.

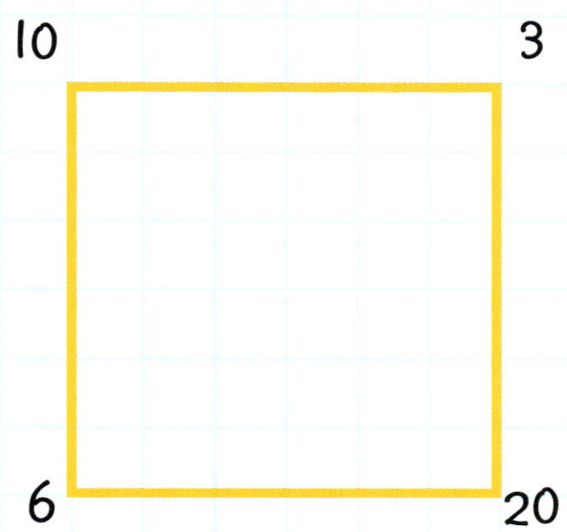

2. Mark the middle of one side of the square.

3. Find the difference between the two numbers at the corners of that side. Write the answer next to your mark.

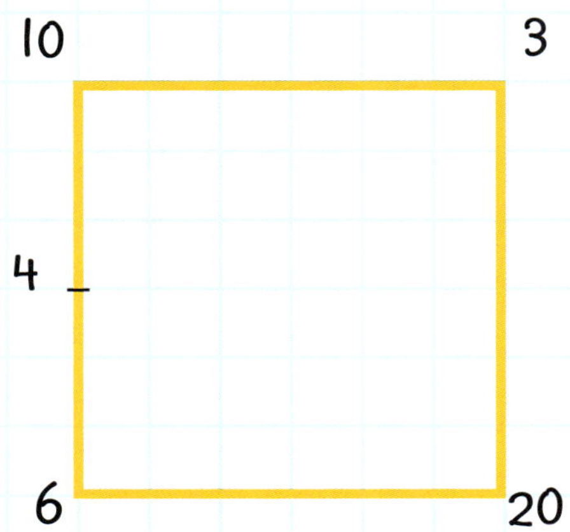

4. Repeat step 3 on the other three sides of your square.

5. Join up your marks to make a smaller square inside your first one.

6. Just as you did on the the big square, mark the middle of each side and write in the differences.

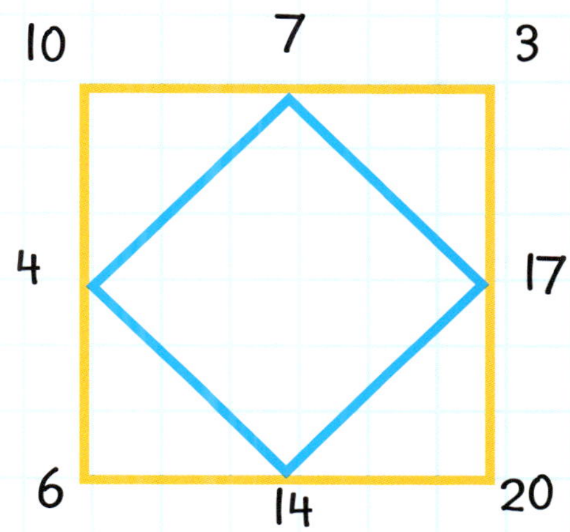

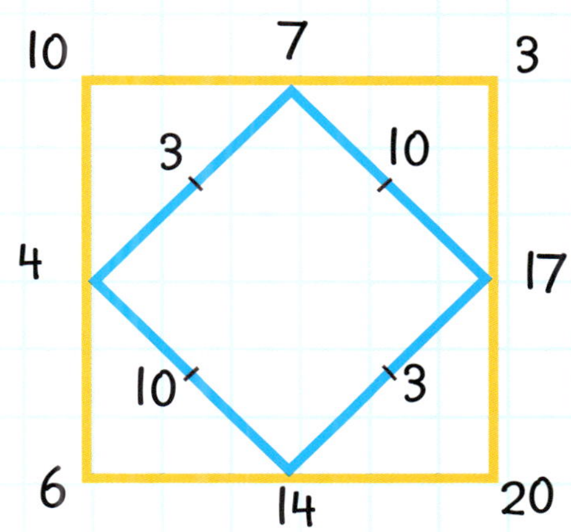

7. Keep going. What happens?

Start again, and try with a different set of numbers. Does the same thing happen again?

Four in a Row

Get Ready

You will need:
- Counters in two colors
- Two paper clips
- A friend to play with

1. Each player takes a set of counters and uses them to play the game on the track and board on page 25. The players decide who goes first and that player picks up the two paper clips.

2. Player One puts a paper clip on two of the numbers on the track.

   For example, 2 and 5:

1	2	3	4	5	6	7	8	9

   If you wish, you can put both paper clips on the same number.

3. Player One adds the two numbers.

4. If the answer is on the board, Player One covers it with a counter.

15	17	8	13	11
9	10	14	8	4
7	13	18	12	9
10	11	5	3	7
16	6	10	2	12

5. Player Two moves ONE of the paper clips to a different number on the track. They add the two numbers and, if they can, cover that number on the board with a counter.

   (If the sum of the two numbers is already covered, the player cannot put a counter on the board.)

6. The players carry on taking turns.

   The winner is the player to put four counters in a row on the board — vertically, horizontally, or diagonally!

1	2	3	4	5	6	7	8	9

15	17	8	13	11
9	10	14	8	4
7	13	18	12	9
10	11	5	3	7
16	6	10	2	12

Nice & Nasty

This card game can be played NICE or NASTY! Each player tries to make the largest 3-digit number.

Get Ready

You will need:

- A pack of playing cards with just the 1 to 9 cards (Aces count as 1)
- A friend to play with

To Play Nice

1. Shuffle, or mix up, the cards and put them facedown in a pile.
2. Player One turns over the top card. They put the card faceup on one of the spaces on their board on page 27.

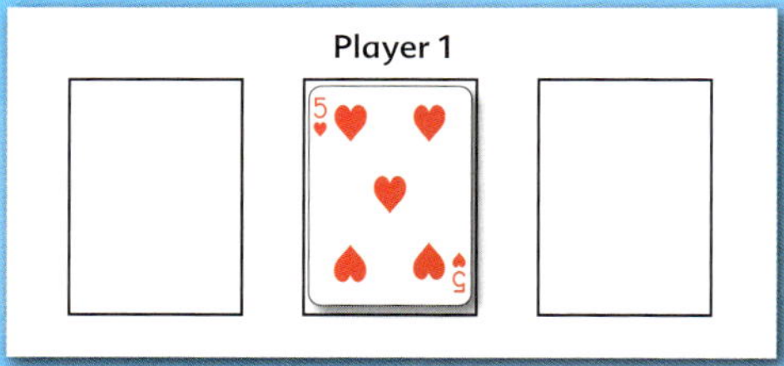

3. Player Two turns over the next card. They put the card faceup on their board.

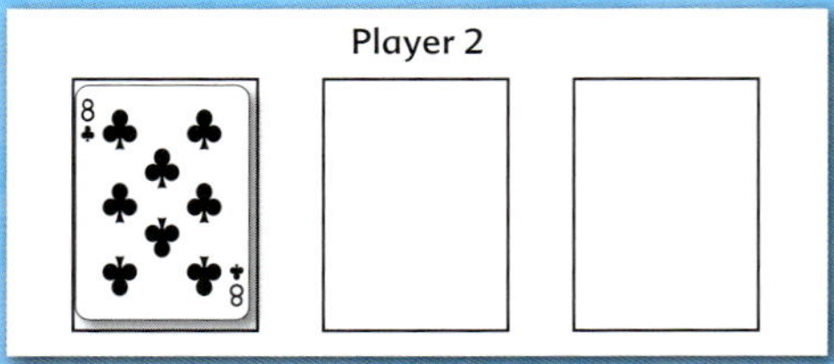

4. The players continue taking turns until all six spaces are filled. Here, Player One has made 951. Player One wins!

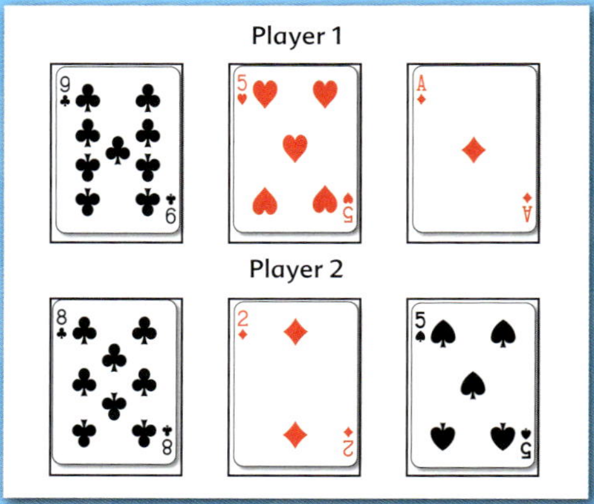

5. Put the six cards back in the pack, shuffle the cards and start again. The winner is the first player to score 5 points!

To Play Nasty

This game is just like Nice, but now each player can either place their card on their own spaces or place it on their opponent's board.

The players continue taking turns. If one player's board gets filled first, then both players must lay their cards on the other board.

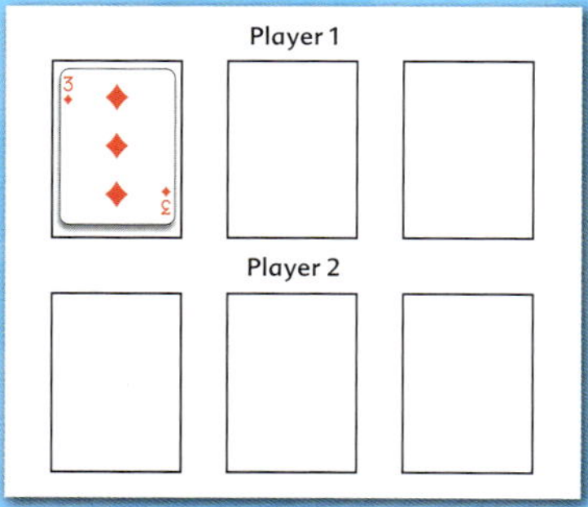

Player 1

Player 2

Silly Stories

Who can make up the silliest mathematics story problem?

Get Ready

You will need:

- 4 counters
- A die
- A friend to play with

1. Roll the die. Use the score to decide who will be the characters in your story. Place a counter next to those characters.

Who

1. King and queen
2. Brother and sister
3. Cat and dog
4. Princess and dragon
5. Elephant and mouse
6. Horse and rider

2. Roll the die again. Use the score to decide where your story takes place.

Where

1. At a farm
2. By the seaside
3. In a boat
4. Under the sea
5. In a castle
6. At the supermarket

3. Roll the die again. Use the score to decide what the characters are doing.

What

1. Baking a cake
2. Bouncing a ball
3. Washing plates
4. Having a race
5. Eating toast
6. Jumping up and down

4. Roll the die again. Use the score to decide what mathematical word or words have to be in your story.

Maths Words

1. Plus
2. Minus
3. Add
4. Take away
5. Altogether
6. Difference

5 Roll the die one last time. The score on the die has to be the answer to a problem in your story.

You and your friend now have 2 minutes to each make up a silly story problem. Decide whose story problem was sillier and that person scores a point!

Here is an example of a silly story:

Princess and dragon (roll 4)

At the supermarket (roll 6)

Eating toast (roll 5)

Altogether (roll 5)

Answer to the problem is 3

Once upon a time, a princess had a pet dragon. The princess loved toast, so she took the dragon to the supermarket to buy bread. The dragon used its fiery breath to toast 2 slices of bread. But the princess was still hungry. So the dragon toasted another slice of bread. How many slices of bread did the dragon toast altogether?

The answer is 3.

Tips for Math Success

Page 4: Ladybug, Ladybug

This activity will help learners understand odd and even numbers. They can also try picking up a handful of counters and predict whether or not they can split them evenly.

Page 5: Zigzag Numbers

Seeing how odd and even numbers alternate will help deepen learners' understanding of this math concept. They can also try making strips that start at different numbers, for example from 10 or 100.

Page 6: Shape Numbers

Square and triangular numbers both come up in lots of later mathematics. Therefore, having a sense of these numbers by making them with counters gives learners a sound grounding for later work. Apart from 1, the first number to be both square and triangular is 36.

Page 7: Let's Play Pick Up

This game will help learners develop strategic thinking. After playing the game a few times, they should get a sense that if they get to pick up the seventh object they are sure to win. You can try playing the game with only seven objects to explore the winning position with this many counters. Learners should discover that if you pick up the fourth object, you are sure to pick up the seventh and win. And then if you pick up the first object, you are sure to pick up the fourth and seventh. It turns out that whoever goes first can always win Pick Up!

Page 8: Pick Up 6

After you have played this a few times, learners should realize the fact that some totals come up more often than others, 7 being the most likely. You could work with them on the number of different ways that you can score 7 with the two dice compared with, say, scoring 11. Learners should be able to explain why putting a counter on 1 is not a good idea.

Page 9: Combine 4

The calculations here are not too difficult. Learners may lose track, however, of which calculations they've done, so help them to be systematic in their working. Try recording each calculation on a separate slip of paper. Then the pieces of paper can be sorted to make a string of numbers in order.

$6 + 5 - 2 = 9$

$2 + 3 + 5 = 10$

$2 + 3 + 6 = 11$

By adding and subtracting all four 4s, it's possible to make 16, 8, and 0.

Pages 10–11: Dartboard Challenge

These games give learners plenty of adding practice and also the challenge of looking for many different solutions.

Pages 12–13: Domino Challenge

As well as being a great game, dominoes have lots of potential for practicing addition and subtraction.

You can mystify learners with this "trick," which they can then try out on their friends. Secretly hide one domino from a full set of 28. Write down the two numbers from the hidden piece. Now ask them to make a long domino train, using all the pieces and matching them in the usual way by adjoining numbers that are the same. The two numbers at the ends of the train will match the secret numbers you've written down.

Page 14: Let's Make 10

Learners should be confident at knowing the number bonds to 10 (the pairs of numbers that make 10 exactly).
This activity provides plenty of practice.

Page 15: Let's Play Fish

Playing Fish is another great way to practice the number bonds to 10, with the added twist of having to remember the positions of the cards.

Page 16: Magic Dice

This trick helps learners practice subtracting a small number from 21.
If they are confident with this, they can do the trick with four dice. This time, they must subtract the top number from 28.

Page 17: Number Poem

This activity is a fun chance for learners to be creative about where numbers occur in their everyday life or in the world around them.

Page 18: What's Your Name's Number?

Some of the numbers here might be too big for learners to easily add.
In those cases it's fine for them to use the calculator on your phone. The important thing here is about the different sizes of the answers, so do not get bogged down in doing the addition.

Page 19: Five Steps to 50

Being able to add or subtract 1 or 10 to or from a number is a key math skill.
This activity provides plenty of practice.

Page 20: Five a Side

A key thing here is to encourage learners to find a way to record their solutions and to persevere at finding as many solutions as possible.

There are 20 solutions altogether, when you allow for zero to be included. The smallest number of counters needed is 8 and the largest is 15.

Page 21: Make 15

There is a way of arranging the nine cards so that every row, column, and diagonal add up to 15. It is unlikely that learners will find this solution, but if they are interested to try this challenge, here are some examples of the answers they might find. This type of arrangement of numbers is known as a Magic Square.

4	9	2
3	5	7
8	1	6

8	1	6
3	5	7
4	9	2

6	1	8
7	5	3
2	9	4

Page 22: At the Corners

Putting numbers into triangles or squares will help learners become confident in thinking about adding three or four small numbers. If they find the activity easy, encourage them to try a larger number in the center of the triangle or square.

Page 23: What's the Difference?

This activity is a great way to practice subtraction. All the answers eventually reduce to zero, motivating learners to try larger numbers to see if it still works.

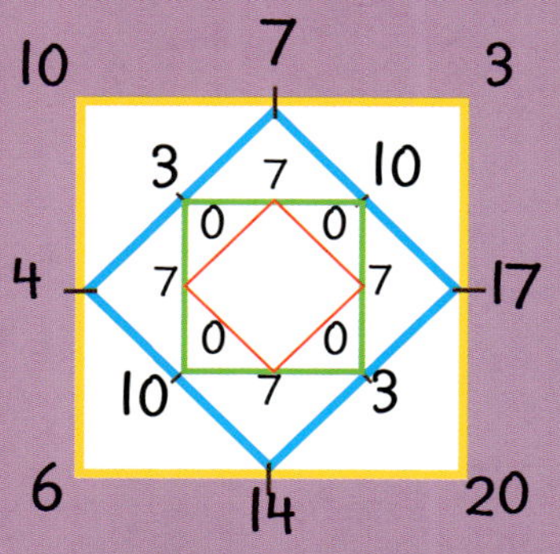

Pages 24–25: Four in a Row

This game provides practice in adding. It also involves strategic thinking as players not only have to try to create their own line of four, but also try to block their opponent.

Pages 26–27: Nice & Nasty

Both versions of this game are about ordering three-digit numbers, but the nasty version adds a twist that learners love. Talk about whether at any point in the game they know for certain who has won before both numbers are complete.

Pages 28–29: Silly Stories

Being able to carry out calculations is important. However, learners also need to know when a calculation might be used. They should also be able to confidently use the different terms for addition and subtraction. This activity provides a light-hearted way to play with both of these skills.